ALLEN PHOTOGRAPHIC GUIDES

PREPARING FOR THE TOWING TEST

CONTENTS

REGULATIONS 2

PRACTISING 3

EYESIGHT 4

VEHICLES AND TRAILERS 4

MANUAL OR AUTOMATIC 5

TEST FORMAT AND MARKING 5

REVERSE EXERCISE 6

MANOEUVRING-AREA LAYOUT 6

REVERSING STEP-BY-STEP 8

PRACTISING AT 10

BRAKING TEST 11

PRACTISING 12

THE DRIVE 12

PULLING AWAY 12

SPEED 14

MEETING POINTS 14

TURNING 15

SAFE FOLLOWING 15

LANE DISCIPLINE 15

ROUNDABOUTS 16

CONSIDERATION 17

UNCOUPLING AND RECOUPLING 18

PRE-TEST CHECKLIST 22

CONTACTS 23

FURTHER READING 23

GW00648942

Until 1997 you could take your driving test in a Mini and the next day take to the road, alone, in a vehicle and trailer outfit weighing several tonnes. The towing vehicle could even be a minibus full of children but the law required no experience, training or qualifications beyond the normal driving test.

With our roads getting busier, and the European Union demanding harmonization of driving tests and licences, that had to change so new driving licence categories and entitlements were introduced for anyone who passed their test after 1 January 1997. *It must be stressed that these changes do not affect anyone who passed their test before that date.*

The 'Horse Sense' boxes throughout the book emphasize special considerations in horsy situations not covered by the test.

REGULATIONS

Anyone who has passed their driving test since 1 January 1997 is allowed to drive vehicles up to 3.5 tonnes MAM with a trailer up to 750 kg MAM. However, they can tow a heavier braked trailer with a lighter car as long as the outfit's MAM is no more than 3.5 tonnes and the trailer's MAM is less than the car's unladen weight. If your trailer's MAM is very close to the car's kerb weight, it may be sensible to take the test to avoid becoming a legal test case!

It is important to realize it is the trailer's MAM that matters, not its actual weight at the time, so you cannot even tow it empty.

This means you need to take a towing test to tow almost all horse trailers. Most double horse trailers have MAMs over two tonnes so have the potential to weigh more than all but the

WHAT DOES THAT MEAN?

Outfit: the vehicle and trailer together.

MAM: maximum authorised mass, which is the maximum weight for a trailer or car laid down by the manufacturer. Also called gross weight or maximum laden weight.

Unladen weight: the legislation uses this term though it strictly means the car without any of the fluids necessary to drive it. As cars do not even leave the production line empty, car manufacturers quote kerb weight, which includes the fluids and, often, an allowance for a driver, so that is the weight used in practice.

Maximum towing weight: this is the maximum weight a car can tow as laid down by the car manufacturer.

DVLA: Driver and Vehicle Licensing Agency; the Government body responsible for issuing licences and registering vehicles.

DSA: Driving Standards Agency; the Government body responsible for driving tests and driver education matters.

B+E: the licence category you need to tow larger trailers. B is cars up to 3.5 tonnes with up to eight seats and E is the trailer. The towing test is officially the B+E test.

heaviest off-roaders and almost all outfits would exceed the 3.5 tonne maximum.

Post 1997 drivers are also limited to vehicles with up to eight seats, so to drive vehicles with nine to nineteen seats they must have two years experience and pass a minibus test. A minibus towing test must then be passed to tow anything weighing more than 750 kg MAM and even then these drivers are only allowed to tow trailers whose MAM is less than the minibus' unladen

weight. This includes the Land Rover Defender 110 Stationwagon and some double horse trailers have MAMs higher than this capable tow-car's unladen weight (*above*). Those who pass the standard towing test can use any other Defender version with trailers up to its 3.5 tonne maximum towing weight.

WEIGHING IT UP

The weight limits in the towing regulations are sensible. Car manufacturers quote a maximum towing weight for each model which is based on its ability to pull away on a slope and is no guarantee of towing safety. Towing experts and the DSA's *Driving* manual recommend keeping the trailer's actual weight to 85 per cent of the car's kerb weight. The closer the trailer gets to the car's weight, the more careful you must be, but a trailer weighing more than the car has the potential to be the tail wagging the dog.

PRACTISING

Post-1997 drivers are allowed to practise towing on the road if they display L-plates and are accompanied by someone aged over twenty-one who has had the B+E entitlement for at least three years, which includes anyone who passed

their driving test before 1997. You cannot tow anything on a provisional licence.

If you do not comply with this you will be driving without a valid licence for the class of vehicle and therefore uninsured – even if you are insured to drive the car without a trailer. Anyone allowing or asking someone to commit these offences can also be prosecuted. Ignorance is no defence because it is up to the driver and anyone who asks them to drive to check that they are entitled and insured to do so. Fines for these offences are high and offenders face increased insurance premiums or may be refused insurance. If you have an accident you may not be able to meet personal injury claims which can run to many thousands of pounds.

Before driving, check the car insurance covers you. Most car insurance gives at least third party cover when towing but while that will pay for the damage your trailer does to others, it will not pay for repairs to the trailer or for its replacement. You can either take out a trailer extension on the car policy or a separate trailer policy. The latter is essential if you tow with more than one car. Also check that the policy does not have any exclusions concerning the driver's qualifications. *Before you take your test you will have to sign a form saying you have suitable insurance.*

PICTURE NOTE

The outfit shown in our photographs did not carry L-plates because it was only driven by people holding the B+E licence category.

EYESIGHT

Test your eyesight now while you still have time to do something about problems. Before the towing test you will be required to read a numberplate from a set distance. If it is the old style plate (*below*) with letters 79.4 mm high you must be able to read it from 20.5 m but the plates introduced in 2001 with two prefix letters (*above right*) must be read from 20 m. If you need glasses or contact lenses to read them, you have to wear them while driving. No other health check is required.

VEHICLES AND TRAILERS

Do not wait until the test to check your vehicle and trailer are suitable and legal, not least because you could be prosecuted if anything were wrong.

For safety, your towing vehicle has to be suitable for the trailer. For the test it must be legally roadworthy, insured, display a valid tax disc and if it is over three years old must have a valid MOT certificate. Check these now and make note of anything expiring before you take the test.

The trailer must also be legally roadworthy. So check tyres, lights and reflectors now and make sure you have a proper, illuminated, legal numberplate that matches the towcar's. Trailers must show two white side lights to the front and the same rear lights as a car (except for the reversing light, which trailers in Britain do not have) plus two triangular red reflectors. All must be working and undamaged.

The test trailer also has to have a MAM of at least a tonne, which makes all horse trailers suitable. You must be able to produce evidence of this, so check it has a chassis plate with the weights shown, or get it in writing from the manufacturer.

The trailer must also have a box-type body, which includes horse trailers.

Failure to comply with any of this on your test day, including arriving with a handwritten 'numberplate', will result in cancellation with no refund.

MANUAL OR AUTOMATIC

Whether you tow with a manual or automatic is largely personal choice but the disadvantage of taking the towing test in an automatic is that an automatic is all you will be allowed to tow with, even if your ordinary licence covers you for manuals. If you pass the test in a manual, you can also tow with an automatic.

TEST FORMAT AND MARKING

There are two parts to the test: manoeuvres carried out at a lorry driving-test centre and about an hour on the road. A braking test is always done before going out on the road and uncoupling and recoupling are usually done on the return to the centre. As with the ordinary driving test since 1 September 2003, the examiner will ask 'show me, tell me' questions on maintenance and safety issues, choosing from a selection of questions, examples of which can be found on the DSA website. Some apply to

the car and others to the trailer, so you might be asked to show how you check brake-fluid level or explain how you check tyres on both parts of the outfit. You will find much of this covered in the *Towing Trailers* and *Trailer Maintenance* guides in this series.

Some questions are irrelevant to horse trailers but a sensible examiner should realize that. For example, one question concerns safe load distribution which, on a cargo trailer, would mean evenly distributing the load over the axles, with heavy objects low down, and securely fastening it. This is not an option with horses!

The examiner has a marking sheet with a series of tick boxes for forty-five aspects of the

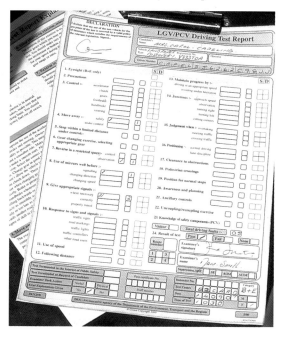

test. Most have a box which is marked each time you show a fault, plus boxes to be ticked in the case of a serious or dangerous fault. A serious fault is something potentially dangerous, like changing lanes without looking. A dangerous fault is where there was actual danger and the examiner may have had to intervene, like a lane change forcing another driver to swerve.

Serious or dangerous faults result in immediate failure, though you continue the test because that is the service you have paid for and it will show you what you need to work on for next time.

Ordinary driving faults are added up at the end of the test and if you get more than fifteen, you fail. Whatever happens, the examiner will debrief you explaining any problems.

REVERSE EXERCISE

Reversing frightens most towing novices, and not-so-novices, but trailer reversing is a vital skill that comes with practice. If you think the test exercise sounds difficult, remember truckers do it with articulated lorries!

MANOEUVRING-AREA LAYOUT

The reversing area is laid out in proportion to the length and width of your outfit. You provide measurements on your application form but if you change the outfit, tell the examiner the new measurements on the day.

All the cones you drive through are 1.5 times the width of the widest part of the outfit's bodywork (excluding mirrors) and the overall length of the manoeuvre is five times the length of the outfit. So, with this 2.12 m by 8.9 m Land Rover Discovery and Ifor Williams HB 505R outfit the bollards are 3.18 m apart and the manoeuvre is 44.5 m long, but with a shorter Land Rover Defender 90 it would be 40 m long. (*See diagram opposite.*)

Cone A1 is 1 m inside the reversing area's boundary line and the distance from cone A to cone B is twice the outfit length.

The bay is based on the outfit's length but can be varied by the examiner by between 1 m over and 2 m under that length. You will not be told the length before you start. At the end of the bay is a 90 cm wide strip painted on the ground.

The examiner will show you a diagram of the manoeuvring area and ask you to drive straight

COURSES

Basic towing skills are taught in courses run by the Caravan Club (01342 336798) and the Camping and Caravan Club (024 7669 4995). People offering towing courses specifically aimed at horse owners and those towing large trailers advertise in the equestrian press and are listed on the Ifor Williams Trailers' website (www.iwt.co.uk). Alternatively, try your local lorry-driving schools because the test is based on the lorry test.

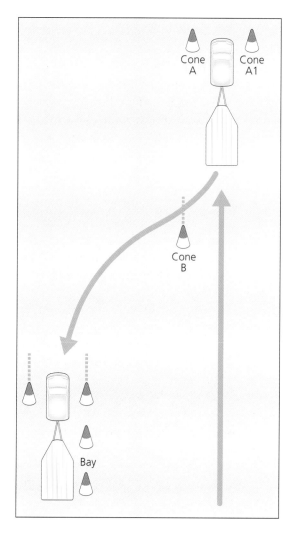

Take it steady: there are no time limits, within reason. You are expected to reverse 'with reasonable accuracy'.

HORSE SENSE

You can assume the test manoeuvring area is a safe one, but when you reverse a trailer in the real world, always: get out to check behind first because it creates a huge blind spot; at shows, get someone to see you back, looking out for riders more interested in their next class than reversing vehicles; when reversing round something you cannot see, like cone B, either get someone to see you back or get out to check its position.

up to the A cones, stopping with the car's nose in line with them. You then reverse to the left of cone B and into the bay, stopping with the back of the trailer over the painted strip. No part of the outfit should go over the boundary line painted around the manoeuvring area. You are not allowed to get out and look once the test has started.

You can pull forwards if it is necessary to get a better view, but not if it is to avoid something – say, because you are about to hit a bollard. The examiner expects to see you observe around the vehicle as if looking out for passers-by, so although you could reverse into the bay by just watching one side of the outfit, he wants to see you checking the other mirror.

REVERSING STEP-BY-STEP

When reversing, you start the trailer turning by steering the opposite way to the direction you want. This is because the front of the car must go right if the back, to which the trailer is attached, is to go left, which turns the trailer's rear right. Some people find it helps if they hold the bottom of the steering wheel because their hands then move in the direction the trailer is going. However, once the trailer is going in the desired direction you have to steer back the other way or it will carry on tightening its turn until it jackknifes. Once it does that you have to pull forwards to straighten it, which will not help your pass chances. The point at which you change steering direction and the amount of steering-wheel movement required to keep it straight is something you can only learn through experience.

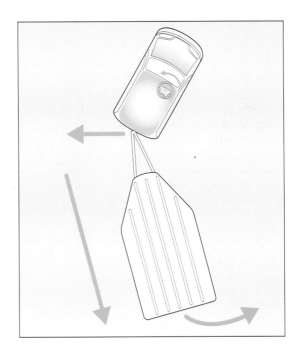

1. Approach the A cones straight and aim to stop in the position shown. The examiner may ask you to move forwards or backwards

and will ask you to realign the outfit if cone B cannot be seen from cone A. Do not get too close to cone A1 or the front right wheel may swing over the boundary line as you move back.

2. Immediately on moving back, turn the steering to the right to start the trailer turning left. You must turn quite sharply, being careful not to jackknife or swing out over the boundary line. If cone B was visible in the passenger door mirror, it soon

disappears and cannot be seen from the driver's side until the last moment as the outfit straightens.

3. Now go almost straight back, diagonally across the area, aiming the driver's side of the trailer at the right-hand cone of the bay entrance, checking the passenger door mirror as you go.

4. The bay entrance is wide enough to go through at a slight angle, steering left to bring the trailer round.

5. If you put the trailer at a slight angle in the bay it will be easier to judge when its back end is over the painted area. No part of the trailer must go beyond the painted area, so remember the ramp feet stick out!

PRACTISING AT HOME

Do not try the test manoeuvre until you have mastered basic reversing skills. Start by reversing to the right and in a straight line, because they are easiest. Reversing left becomes easier once you get a feel for how the trailer turns. It pays to have someone outside the car observing what you are doing but, if you are not using a professional tutor, pick someone patient. Once they have helped you with the basics, just keep practising.

Do not aimlessly reverse around a field, but use lightweight items to mark areas to reverse into – plastic buckets, feed bags and electric-fence Polyposts do no damage if struck.

Once confident, practise the separate elements required for the test.

1. Get someone to direct you up to two objects in line so you can see what it looks like from the driving seat, then try to achieve the same without help. Move the objects around the field so you cannot use landmarks to help.

2. Reverse to the left around a marker placed the correct distance from the starting point.

Pay particular attention to avoiding the point at which the outfit jackknifes and to trying to get it back into line as you pass the object.

3. Reverse in a straight line. Most people find this easier using the mirrors alone. When more of the trailer appears in one mirror than the other, turn the steering wheel towards that mirror. It is better to make small steering movements frequently than risk over-correction from which recovery is harder.

4. Use feed bags to create a 90 cm wide marker on the ground and reverse up to it from varying distances. Aim to get the bags' leading edge halfway between the back of the trailer and the rear wheels, which ensures the back end is well over the test area's painted patch without risking projecting beyond it.

5. Finally, practise the whole manoeuvre.

BRAKING TEST

This is not an emergency stop but shows you can stop as quickly and safely as possible, under control and in a straight line. You will be penalised for harsh braking, especially if it causes skidding of car or trailer, but you will also be marked down for taking too long to stop.

The examiner asks you to stop 61 m from two cones, then asks you to drive forwards, reaching at least

20 mph before braking as you pass between the cones. Aim for between 20 and 30 mph and brake firmly, being careful not to anticipate the markers and to depress the clutch as you come to a halt so the engine does not stall.

PRACTISING

The best place to practise braking is off the road, but it must be on a safe, paved surface. If you take lessons at a lorry-driving school they will have suitable facilities, but if you must use a road, find somewhere very quiet and pull over if other vehicles appear – they will not expect you to brake for no apparent reason!

Do not practise this for too long because it could overheat the car and trailer brakes, reducing their efficiency.

you learned for your ordinary driving test. We are not going to cover everything in those books, only aspects with particular relevance to towing.

HORSE SENSE

This is the sort of braking you would try to avoid with horses aboard because it causes them discomfort and stress. By looking and thinking ahead you should be able to keep sudden, hard braking to a minimum.

PULLING AWAY

You must use the mirror and signal before pulling away as well as being careful not to roll back or stall. The car needs more power to pull away with a trailer than solo, but do not over-rev it. Again, practice makes perfect.

THE DRIVE

You are expected to drive at least to the standard of the ordinary driving test but you will not do the emergency stop, reverse parking, reversing round a corner or turning in the road (three-point turn).

There will be great emphasis on observation and effective use of the mirrors. You must show you are aware of what the trailer is doing, especially at the times when there are particular considerations caused by towing. For example, the way the trailer follows a tighter line than the car round corners.

Read the latest editions of the *Highway Code* and the DSA's *Driving* manual to refresh your memory on the rules of the road and basic skills

Because the trailer follows a tighter line than the car in any turn, you have to turn out more than in a solo car, especially if you are pulling around a parked car or out of a lay-by. That can take the towcar to the wrong side, even on quite wide roads, so do not get a mirror fixation because your examiner expects to see you watching traffic in both directions!

If your towcar has a rev counter, you can use it to help you practise pulling away smoothly. Find out the engine speed in revolutions per minute at which it develops peak torque (pulling power shown in pounds-feet [lb ft] or Newton metres [Nm]). In first gear with the clutch depressed, push the throttle pedal until the rev counter needle is around that point. Then, instead of juggling two pedals, hold the throttle steady and slowly raise the clutch pedal, using clutch adjustments alone to keep the needle around peak torque rpm as the car moves off. As the clutch eventually becomes fully engaged, depress the throttle to accelerate away.

You should soon get a feel for pulling away on the flat without resorting to this method, but remember it for pulling away on steep hills.

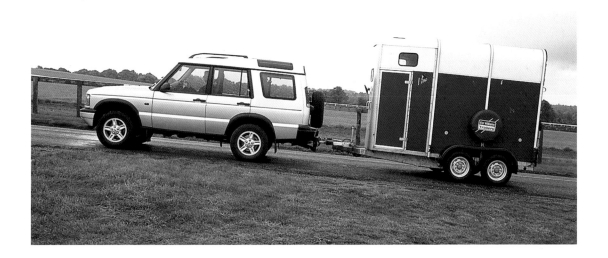

SPEED

Treat speed limits as maximums and drive at a safe speed for the situation. However, you can be marked down for driving too slowly as well as for speeding.

Unless lower limits are shown on road signs, see right for the towing speed limits.

30 Urban roads

50 Rural single carriageways

60 Dual-carriageways and motorways

MEETING POINTS

You are expected to meet other vehicles safely so it is important to remember not everyone will notice the trailer and, sometimes, cannot be expected to see it. You must allow more time for coming out of junctions, not least because if you get it wrong, hedges and walls may stop oncoming drivers seeing the trailer about to fill the space they plan to use! Motorcyclists are especially vulnerable to this.

Take care when passing parked cars because drivers getting out or pulling out may see the towcar and not the trailer – using lights in crowded town streets reduces the risk. The same applies to drivers joining main roads from slip roads. You will not fail your test for a polite horn warning.

A car and trailer need more time and space than a solo car to pull round an obstacle so do not pull to the wrong side of the road if you would baulk oncoming traffic. However, let others go first rather than squeezing through a gap because you have right of way.

TURNING

Trailers always turn tighter than the towcar and the sharper the corner, the tighter they turn. Turn wide, but keep an eye on the inside mirror, especially on bends with obstructions like traffic lights. In spite of their vulnerability, cyclists are the most likely to get into the space you allow for turning, so check for them and be prepared to stop. If turning near pedestrians, allow more room, if possible, in case they step off the kerb, not realizing the trailer will be closer than the car.

Take care when turning left into narrow roads because you may have to go to the wrong side to get round.

When turning right, check mirrors, signal and pull to the centre of the road as early as possible, stopping so the nose of the car is just short of the centre line of the road you are turning into. Before turning, check the mirror again in case anyone is overtaking in spite of your signal! Turn, aiming the car close to the nearside kerb so the trailer has room to turn in without cutting across the white line. If anyone is waiting to come out of the road you are turning into, it may be safer to let them out first.

SAFE FOLLOWING

You are expected to keep a safe following distance. If you keep a minimum two-second gap between you and the vehicle in front, you will have time to react if something goes wrong and not have to judge what, say, 50 m looks like at 50 mph. Start saying 'Only a fool forgets the two-second rule', at normal speaking pace, as the car in front passes a landmark and if you have finished before you arrive at the object, you are more than two seconds behind. Allow more room in rain or poor visibility.

LANE DISCIPLINE

Check mirrors carefully and signal well before changing lanes. It can be difficult to judge how close an overtaking car is to the back of the trailer so, if in doubt, let them pass.

In multi-lane roads you must keep to the left unless overtaking. Towcars are not allowed into the right-hand lane on motorways with three or more lanes, but can use that lane on an ordinary dual carriageway.

In one-way streets and when approaching junctions you must use the appropriate lane for your exit. Allow more time to move over because you need more space to do so.

ROUNDABOUTS

It is especially important to use the correct signals at roundabouts when towing because as you need more space than a solo car, other drivers might misinterpret your road position. Good observation is also vital, so constantly check both mirrors and look around you.

As a trailer follows a tighter line than the car, you must allow room on the inside when turning left and for the

island when turning right. Unfortunately, other road users do not always understand this, so look out for people trying to get into the space you have allowed.

Also beware of drivers entering the roundabout quickly and not judging their speed in relation to yours. If you are already on the roundabout, you have right of way but, while you should not be intimidated by their misuse of the horn, you also have the responsibility to avoid accidents and will fail if you have one.

HORSE SENSE

Roundabouts must be taken slowly with horses aboard because they often find it difficult to cope with the changes in direction, especially after a long, straight stretch.

CONSIDERATION

You are expected to show consideration for others throughout the test. Pass pedestrians, cyclists and motorcyclists wide and be prepared to slow down in case the extra turbulence from the trailer takes them by surprise.

Driving past horses needs special care because they are often upset by the trailer's rattling and sometimes seem surprised by a car having something on the back. They often react more strongly to a trailer with a horse aboard.

In traffic jams do not pull forwards unless you are sure the trailer will clear junctions and pedestrian crossings.

If traffic backs up behind you, consider signalling and pulling over in a safe place to let them past.

UNCOUPLING AND RECOUPLING

The examiner wants to see you use a safe sequence so you forget nothing. You will not fail if, say, you undo the breakaway cable before unplugging the lights, but you will if you unhitch before applying the trailer handbrake. If you use a stabilizer you must remove and refit it, so it may be easier to leave it at home.

Tell the examiner if you have disabilities that prevent you from carrying out any part of this exercise.

The uncoupling sequence the DSA suggests is:

1. Stop on safe, level ground and ensure the handbrakes are applied on the car and trailer.

2. Drop and lock the jockey wheel.

3. Disconnect and safely stow the electrical plug, then remove the stabilizer, if fitted.

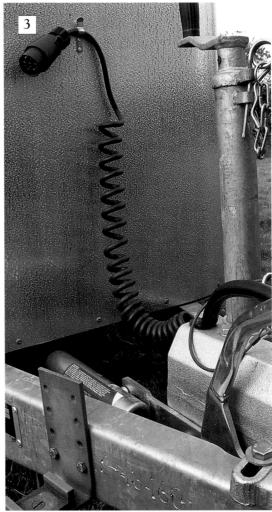

4. Unclip and stow the break-away cable.

5. Unhitch by raising the jockey wheel while holding the hitch's unlocking handle.

6. You must then pull forwards before reversing back to park alongside the trailer.

The suggested recoupling method is:

1. Reverse up to the trailer and apply the handbrake.

2. Lower the hitch onto the towball with the jockey wheel, holding the locking handle up, if the hitch requires it.

3. Check the hitch has locked on by raising it with the jockey wheel, then fully raise and lock the wheel.

4. Attach the breakaway cable. It must go to a suitably strong point or a purpose-made attachment point, if the towbar has one.

5. Refit the stabilizer and plug in the electrics.

6. Check everything is properly stowed and fitted.

7. Check the car handbrake is on and release the trailer's handbrake.

8. Check the lights work – do the indicators separately, not with the hazard warning switch which is on a different circuit.

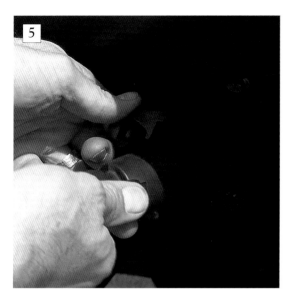

HITCHING AID

The Equibrand Trailer Coupling Mirror allows the driver to see the hitch and ball coming together. The DSA says that there is nothing to stop you using fittings which aid coupling. Equibrand is on 01327 262444.

- [ ] Fuel
- [ ] Matching, legal numberplates
- [ ] L-plates
- [ ] Lubricate locks, hitches and towball
- [ ] Safely stow trailer breach and breast bars
- [ ] Trailer ramps and doors fastened
- [ ] Jockey wheel properly stowed
- [ ] Breakaway cable and electrical plug properly connected
- [ ] Check car and trailer lights (take spare bulbs)
- [ ] Trailer handbrake off
- [ ] Driving licence
- [ ] MOT certificate

PRE-TEST CHECKLIST

- [ ] Car and trailer tyres for faults and pressures
- [ ] Car coolant, screenwash, oil, brake fluid and battery

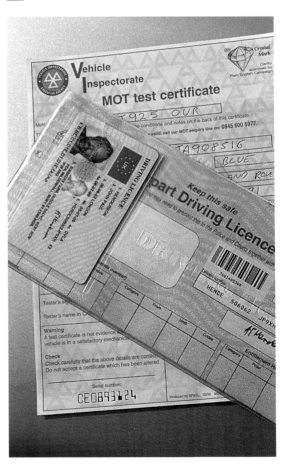

☐ Proof of trailer's weight (chassis plate or letter from manufacturer)

☐ Glasses or contact lenses, with spares

☐ Keys and locking handles for hitch and stabilizer

☐ Wheelbrace and jack for trailer

CONTACTS

Driver and Vehicle Licensing Agency Driver inquiries: 0870 2400009. Vehicle inquiries: 0870 2400010. Website: www.dvla.gov.uk.

Driving Standards Agency Local offices in the phone book. Website: www.driving-tests.co.uk.

Ifor Williams Trailers' website www.iwt.co.uk and the **National Trailer and Towing Association's** site at www.ntta.co.uk have general information about towing and the law.

FURTHER READING

Allen Photographic Guides: *Towing Trailers* and *Trailer Maintenance*.

The Stationery Office: the *Driver Licensing Information* pamphlet sent with your licence and *Driving, The Official Driving Test* and *The Highway Code* available from bookshops.

Society of Motor Manufacturers and Traders' publications department (020 7235 7000): *The SMMT Guide to Towing and the Law.*

ACKNOWLEDGEMENTS

My thanks to: Paul Colliss, supervising staff instructor at the DSA
Training and Development Centre, Cardington, Beds., for information,
guidance and help with test centre photography; Land Rover for the loan
of a Discovery TD5; Ifor Williams Trailers and the DVLA for guidance.

British Library Cataloguing-in-Publication Data.
A catalogue record for this book is available from the British Library

ISBN 0.85131.880.0

Published in Great Britain in 2003 by
J. A. Allen an imprint of Robert Hale Ltd.,
Clerkenwell House, 45–47 Clerkenwell Green,
London EC1R 0HT

Design and Typesetting by Paul Saunders
Series editor Jane Lake
Diagrams by Rodney Paull
Colour processing by Tenon & Polert Colour Processing Ltd., Hong Kong
Printed in China by Midas Printing International Ltd